Almost a Rainbow

By Joan Walsh Anglund

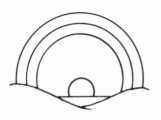

Almost
a
Rainbow

A
Book
of
Poems
by

Joan Walsh Anglund

Random House New York

Library of Congress Cataloging in Publication Data

Anglund, Joan Walsh.

Almost a rainbow.

I. Title.

PS3551.N47A79   811'.54   80-11417

ISBN 0-394-50072-5

Manufactured in the United States of America

02468B97531

IN
LOVING MEMORY
OF
Greg Meredith

Reason
    is the sentinel
        of the mind
  ...but
    the doorway
      to the heart
        is unguarded.

How often
      we kneel
          . . : to our weakness
   when
      we might rise
          . . . to our strength.

Love
is the Rainbow
of each life.

Sometimes
      we love
  that
    which we can
         never understand.

Be as the stars,
    unchanging
        in the firmament,
    Guiding others
        through the darkness
    by your steadfast light.

The brighter
          The day
... The deeper
          The shadow.

Walk carefully
among my dreams,
. . . for they are small
. . . and easily crushed.

Life

is not an answer

. . . it is a question.

Each day
has its Sunrise.

Often
        Happiness calls,
    but
            we are too busy
                    to answer.

No man dies

until he is forgotten.

Praise,
    like
        sunlight,
helps
    all
        things
            grow.

Time
     cannot touch
two hearts
     that truly love.

The greatest pain
is the
estrangement
from
one's
true self.

Tomorrow,
            we shall be older,
      ...but
            shall we
                  be
                        wiser?

I wanted
        to remain
                beautiful
                        for you,
but
the
                mirror
                        is
                        unrelenting,
and
the
                daily
                      "etching"
                                continues.

We hide
        our deepest
            sorrow,
and
        parade,
            instead,
                our smaller woes!

The mind reasons
...the heart knows.

Life
    promises
        only
            Opportunity.

How often
        we are listening
                to yesterday,
when today
        stands ready
                to speak.

As a Lamp
    gives forth Light
So let your heart
    give forth Love,
. . . never asking
    upon which Life
        its illumination
         may fall.

The unveiling
of
one's soul
is
the reason
for
existence

The giving hand
receives.

Through Pain
 . . . we learn,
through Love
 . . . we are reborn.

Fill your heart
        with Beauty,
                and
                        Beauty
                    will come to you.
Fill your thoughts
        with Love,
                and
                        Love surrounds you.
Seek always Truth
        and it shall be
                yours.
For
        as you believe
        are all things
                made manifest
                    unto you.

Forgive the Past
   . . . he tried!

There are not
        separate loves,
... there is only
    One love
... from which
    we all partake.

Even
        as the flowers of the spring,
and the trees of the forest
        ...all Life
                reaches
                        toward the Light.
Reach always
                for the Light
        ...it is your source,
For all things
                melt away
as do the winter snows...
                        ...and in the end
                                there is
                                only
                                        Love.